AF333061

SONNETS FROM THE MARE IMBRIUM

Sonnets from the Mare Imbrium

Bart Baxter

FLOATING BRIDGE PRESS

Acknowledgments

Grateful acknowledgment is given to the publications in which the following poems, some in slightly altered versions, first appeared:

The Formalist: "Detective Work"
Poetry: "The Magician's Beautiful Assistant," "Compulsories," and "Florence (iii)"
Peace for the Arsonist: "Lichen," "Sunday at the Tide Pool," and "Tableau"
Pontoon I, An Anthology of Washington State Poets: "On First Looking into Moncrieff's Proust"
Rain Magazine: "On the Twenty-First Birthday of Vincenzio Galilei"

©1999 by Floating Bridge Press
ISBN 0-9647199-7-5

The printing of this chapbook was supported, in part, by grants from Allied Arts Foundation, and Seattle Arts Commission.

Cover linoleum cut designed by Jules Remedios Faye.

Editors: T. Clear, Jeff Crandall, Linda Greenmun,
Peter Pereira and Gary Winans

Floating Bridge Press
PO Box 18814
Seattle, Washington 98118
www.scn.org/arts/floatingbridge

for my daughter

CONTENTS

The Magician's Beautiful Assistant

She pushes up her chest a little, tries
to rearrange her top, makes some pretense
of bending at the waist to help disguise
his old illusions, and the audience
plays right along. They never see the doves
under the handkerchief, the six of hearts
behind his back, and as for him, he loves
to watch her, too. Sometimes he fumbles, starts
wondering if it's really him they've come
to see. Her sleight of hand has made it hard
to tell. After the show she takes him home
with her. She asks him if he'll pick a card,
but not just any card: the one that won't
be done with now you see it, now you don't.

FLORENCE (i)

The clouds parade in dress whites. Uniform
facades banner the noon, and now and then
a red Lambretta mutters by within
earshot. Some share bruschetta on the warm
loggia where doves coo, and a ladder leans
against old brickwork. History careers
like scooters on cobblestone, shifting gears
to speed up or slow down uncertain scenes.
Across this ancient river then, like art
or after-dinner drinks, I know you wait,
not necessarily for me, but for
someone (who might as well be me). Your part
is harbor, gallery, compassionate
reminder of the feast and the boudoir.

FLORENCE (ii)

She comes down to the shore as if she comes
to the piazza, looking for someone
she knows or thinks she knows. She sees the sun
over the cypress trees and Christendom's
most garish architecture, wondering
if Savonarola might have stood here
by himself, grimacing at his own fear
where months before he had stood thundering
against the Renaissance. I've thought a lot
about you, some nights more than others. I'd
forgotten what it feels like, and I seem
to be remembering it all, like what
Savonarola said before he died:
that men are no better than what they dream.

FLORENCE (iii)

Sometimes I wake up, and the morning lies
as flat as fresco, like Cimabue's
panels, or stained glass in the Uffizi.
She takes my face between her hands and tries
to model me in the way that *her* eyes
look at the world. What is it she can see
that no one's ever seen before in me?
A figure? Something she can recognize?
A little like Giotto, when he wrapped
his rufous sunlight half around the face
of the Madonna, lovingly and apt,
so not to render her within a place
where (like me) she might be forever trapped,
but letting her step forward into space.

VIRGA

The eyes imagining the presence of
a lover in the empty room, the sound
of promises made, unrequited love,
the little boy whose feet don't touch the ground
when he climbs up into the biggest chair,
the way I try but never quite explain
myself, and I remember how the air
smelled dry as mescal, waiting for the rain
to settle, and how you took me to some
hole-in-the-wall, and we danced, and the sky
was empty like the bar. "It's going to come,"
I heard you whisper. "No matter how dry
this August is, or where we are, I'll bet
that both of us are going to get wet."

Detective Work

We know the man should not have drowned tonight.
We know this from the way his head was turned,
the awful gash, the bloody towels. We learned
this from his sad expression. Oh, he *might*
have slipped on the tile floor. What do *we* know?
We know this much. He was alive to fill
the tub. And something else. He wasn't ill
because we know he had someplace to go.
His wife has told us everything: the play,
the dinner reservations. If he drowned
at all tonight, it could be that she found
him on the baby sitter Saturday
a week ago. Always suspect the spouse,
but most accidents happen in the house.

After the extravagant meal, he took
his son up to the dusty, candlelit
study, laid hands on the device, and shook
as he allowed the boy to handle it.
He showed him how to maneuver the brass
cylinder, held his face up to the lens
and let him look into the polished glass.
That night he focused the pale light of men's
imaginations. They saw galaxies
expanding, stars exploding, lineaments
of God's face in the moon, the Pleiades,
men's eminence and men's inconsequence.
But so much more can my son see the better
if I can help him understand the latter.

On First Looking into Moncrieff's Proust

If when the veiled remark has lost intent,
or eyes meet with no more intrigue than chance,
or comely summer rains append the bent
of iris, or the apple blossoms dance
and I am unimpressed, late afternoons
with Mme. Swann obtain, the way she vamps
and importunes an old marquis, the moon's
cold coronet, the carriage horse that champs
in rime and wet air. Assignations end,
as they should end, with laughter. After all,
is it a wonder that these words portend
desire more than the subtle rise and fall
of a thin blouse, or that her eyes appear
more cerulean than if she were really here.

ROSE

Her bedroom was in disarray, but there
were these extraordinary smells, like dung
and orchids, dog and lavender. The air
was wet with body odor, ball and tongue
and orifice. I never would have guessed,
when we were on the bed, and Mendelssohn
was on the radio, and we undressed
by the low light of votive candles on
the bedside table, that she was fragile
as bone china, held together with wax
and ribbons, pinions less mechanical
than I imagined. There were hairline cracks
in porcelain, and tangled in our clothes,
a cutting from what was a crystal rose.

The acrobat performs an old routine.
He rides his tiny bicycle above
the crowd on slender cable stretched between
two ancient buildings. I imagine love
a little bit like this, and I must be
the one funambulist without some sense
of balance. Gyros right themselves. But we
are like the juggler and his implements,
intent on constant motion, half afraid
to let ourselves come to a stop. I know
that I need your inertia. If I've stayed
at all upright, it's your love makes it so.
It's like the tumble of the bowling pins
or how the plate is stable when it spins.

ODE TO ST. PAULI GIRL

Confederate of souses, paramour
of all carousers, never sees what I
am in the back alley, bent over, dour
inebriate, fall guy for passersby,
breaking a bottle in a paper sack
over something I should have done or said,
some comeback I should have come up with back
at the bar, but I'm in love with her red
cards and fast horses, bards and beer backs. She's
the one who'll smile if I can't keep the room
from spinning or if my apologies
sound unconvincing. She's the one for whom
my best behavior goes unnoticed while
she graces my intemperance with a smile.

HONEY CARP

She says that I won't even entertain
the notion she might have desires that spring
from fantasy. I'm told that I constrain
her imagination, and anything
that can't be specified empirically
she says I denigrate or make light of.
And then, without thinking, I say that she
needs some solidity, and that I love
the way her skin looks in the candlelight,
the sound her stockings make. She looks at me
as if I hadn't heard a word tonight.
Why can't I understand? Why can't I see
the dragonflies and orchids in her head
and golden fish that swim around her bed?

18

Mare Imbrium

The summer sky was like a pyramid
with a golden vertex. The afternoon
came headlong, a knight-errant lost amid
the heavens, hectoring the orange moon
with a lance of dry air and wings of storm
clouds. I was anxious, but you weren't afraid
of anything, and then you put your arm
around me, held me, asked me why I stayed
away so long. That night in bed you wore
a helmet, whorled and white-horned, so that you
could disregard the fealties I swore,
the promises that you might misconstrue,
and so it is you always leave for dead
the one you love with what you say he said.

When after a short absence, in the time
it takes to apprehend how different
we both have become, I forget if I'm
the one supposed to start the argument.
Kind of like ice skating, we have to do
a few compulsories, like figure eights
or axels, and I can't remember who
begins. Aren't you the one who always waits
for innuendo, or am I the one
who finds the irony in everything?
Do we need any more practice? We've done
this spin more times than needs belaboring.
And so we only stare at one another,
each wondering if it was worth the bother.

Ode to St. Pauli Girl (Reprise)

Across the bar, half an arm's length of pearl
Formica, sits Our Lady of the Lost
and Unable to Walk Straight, chorus girl
in pigtails, Sister of the Double-Crossed,
the Saint of the Misbegotten, the one
who will smile if I spend all night with her
and drink myself into oblivion,
the one who won't forsake me when I slur
my words or let my melancholy get
the best of me. We've made it to last call,
and there's so much I meant to say, so let
me lay my head down next to you, and all
my sins be forgotten, and let me hold
you close because the night is long and cold.

FAITH IS

No more or less, I think, than that I might
divine a tree that will both fascinate
and satisfy on this cold winter's night,
that buttered rum can still alleviate
the silver chill and brume, that days and days
of newspapers will still illuminate
the room (if wet wood won't), and that arrays
of candy canes and Christmas lights await,
to be hung up on houses more in need
of paint than flattery, that I can still
tuck children into bed and even read
the *Dubliners* to anyone who will
listen, and fairest faith has always been
the hope I have of seeing you again.

LICHEN

A wild meander, spread like marly yarn
between the patches of last winter's snow,
turns, knotted on the rock. Above the tarn,
between echelles of ice and indigo,
it stays alive, if only by degree,
throughout the seasons, watching earth prepare
for jubilation, spun where rock and scree
collide with altitude, the chilly air,
the aquatint of seasons' weaving, warp
and weft of mint and wildflower in bloom,
persistent purchase of the steep escarp
where summer takes the mountain like a loom
and crisscrosses the Liberty Ridge with rain,
or suncups ice on days of brighter skein.

EPICEDIUM (i)

> — *for Dan Daugherty*

A young pediatrician carries six
cases of beer, two cases at a time,
to Camp Muir for his birthday party, kicks
steps so all of his buddies make the climb.
And you were wasted, couldn't sleep. The noise,
the goddamn party going on until
the last passed out at two or three, annoys
the hell out of me. And you take a chill,
nothing stays down, you can't get out of bed.
We stayed up, talking incoherently
all night, but nothing helped. I held your head
in my lap. Then I got up quietly
and climbed with the young pediatrician.
I should have stayed with you that morning, Dan.

EPICEDIUM (ii)

And we redressed those failures all in all,
forever taking the most galling routes:
across the ice, along the spalling wall,
the longest pendulum, the deepest chutes.
Easy enough to have laid out your life
with a framing hammer in Bellingham,
taught in junior college, taken a wife
in blue denim. If anything can damn
us to endeavor, then poke out our eyes,
more than ineptitude before a friend,
I don't know what it is. We justify
the most godawful stunts, and in the end
such little amnesty, and such desire
to recompense the ones we most admire.

EPICEDIUM (iii)

Odysseus was just another man
till Polyphemus disemboweled his crew,
but you heard more mad wails and whispers than
a man should ever have to listen to.
You led a team of Japanese, that day
on steep snow, crossed the crux pitch still alive
till someone slipped or rotten ice gave way.
And most likely the rest didn't survive
the fall. But I know you did, pissed and wet
with fear, for hours while the Russians tried
to find your body — never did. I'll bet
that even then you were more terrified
of being found, the burden of failure
more weight than you were willing to endure.

This morning, tide has left an anarchy
of crazy little skimmers weaving in
and out, like drunken wet commuters kin
more to a bumper-car with legs than me.
A wary sanderling is scolding dabs,
uncertain of my thermos. Coffee must
make puffin nervous, too. My dogs distrust
the sea anemone and leap at crabs.
A stoic spiny-lobster ministers
to me. His lessons double and expand
the temple of our tiny universe,
and off the wind, the clouds resemble birch
heavy with snow. A widgeon calls, and sand
crabs scuttle off to bless another church.

TABLEAU

How many times have I arranged these cards?
Why is it nine times out of ten I fail
to turn the card I need till all the hearts
have fallen? Fifty-two factorial:
the permutations seem so limitless.
You watch across the table, placing faces,
familiar tricks, patterns. Pointless,
but so engaging. Where are all the aces,
the red jack, the black six, the diamonds?
I play the whole bad deal out in my head.
I turn another card, a heart, from ones
already played, the discards, and instead
of stalemate, find myself about to run
the deck, believing wrongly I have won.

NOTES

Mare Imbrium, or "Sea of Rains," is the largest dead sea on the moon.
Savonarola, a 15th century Italian reformer, was burned at the stake.
Virga is rain that evaporates before it hits the ground.
Tableau is the layout, in Solitaire, to which one may add cards
    according to suit or denomination.
"Rose," "Honey Carp," "Virga," and "Mare Imbrium" were inspired
    by the paintings of Michael Parkes.
St. Pauli Girl is a very good beer.

ABOUT THE AUTHOR

Bart Baxter was born May 28, 1950 in Sherman, Texas. He earned a Bachelor of Arts with honors from the University of Texas and did his postgraduate studies at Boise State University and the University of Washington. His many awards include the 1994 Hart Crane Award for Poetry, First Place in the 1994 MTV Poetry Grand Slam, and First Place in the 1998 Seattle Poetry Grand Slam. He has published two previous volumes of poetry: *Driving Wrong* by Poetry Around Press, Washington, and *Peace for the Arsonist* by Bacchae Press, Ohio. He is married with two children and lives in Seattle, Washington.

This chapbook was designed in Adobe PageMaker and offset-printed in an edition of 400 on acid-free recycled papers. The typeface is Adobe Garamond. The cover titling was handset in Caslon Old Style, and each cover was letterpress printed on a Colts Armory press by Stern & Faye, Printers.

This is number *RC* of 400.